CREATIVE IDEAS FOR
MACHINE EMBROIDERY

Creative Ideas for Machine Embroidery

Corliss Miller

Quilters' Resource *publications*

First published 1995

Printed and bound in Hong Kong

This edition first published in 1997 for
Quilters' Resource Inc.
P.O. Box 148850
Chicago, IL 60614
Phone: 773 - 278 - 5695

ISBN 0 - 9629056 - 4 - X

A catalogue record of this book is available from
the British Library.

DEDICATION
Tim and Sarah, on behalf of Corliss, would like
to thank and dedicate this book to all her many
friends and colleagues in the embroidery world.

Contents

Introduction

Decorating our homes with textiles and embroidery has a very long historical tradition, starting with the basic need to keep warm and gradually getting more decorative as people had more time. In certain periods it became a status symbol as it showed the wealth of those who could afford such things from professional workshops or later on, in upper and middle-class households, where the ladies had leisure time to indulge in making vast quantities of household linen and hangings. Skill with a needle was considered essential to women's education.

Now the pendulum has swung the other way and we have less time. Many women work, either full or part-time, look after their children and run homes. Time is in short supply but in spite of this more and more people like to make items for their own homes, to impress their personality on it, and they find it relaxing and rewarding.

Most households do now possess a domestic sewing machine, so the aim of this book is to encourage you to get out that sewing machine, that remnant of fabric bought in a sale and never used, together with whatever reels of cotton you have and experiment with some samples. I am sure you will be amazed at what you can achieve and will hopefully be so encouraged that you will make some of the things in the following chapters.

Chapter One
Materials & Equipment

Materials & Equipment

FABRICS

With such a wide variety of fabrics to choose from and ever changing fashions in interior design, it makes sense to use fabrics that are good-tempered and reasonably inexpensive.

The following fabrics are commonly used for machine embroidery and would all be suitable for furnishing:

Calico – this comes in a variety of weights
Cotton fabrics – including polyester-cotton mixes
Silk – this also comes in a variety of weights, from the lightest habotai to heavy silk jersey

Other fabrics popular with machine embroiderers are net, muslin, scrim and felt. There are also many beautiful luxury and special effect fabrics available, such as shot organza, taffeta, metallic foil, lace, lurex, chiffon, satin and velvet. These are widely available from most large department stores as well as from specialist fabric shops.

Most fabrics have the manufacturer's finish still in them when you buy them. Others, especially cottons and calico, may not be pre-shrunk so check when buying. If you are using a fabric that is new to you, test it to see how it reacts when it is washed, dyed, stitched, etc.

Several kinds of Vilene are used in machine embroidery, including iron-on Vilene for appliqué work and pelmet Vilene, which is the heaviest weight available.

For quilting you will need wadding. This comes in various weights and can be cotton, silk or polyester. If you are using it for quilts, cushion covers or tablemats, choose a wadding which will stand up to washing as these items need to be washed regularly to keep them fresh and clean.

It is also possible to make up your own fabrics. Small special-effect areas can be created by trapping scraps of thread and fabric in a sandwich of hot or cold dissolvable fabric and machine stitching the whole piece. This can be very dense or fine, depending upon the effect you want to achieve. The pieces can then be used either by applying them to highlight certain areas or inlaid.

Opposite: A wide variety of fabrics can be used for machine embroidery. A few are shown here.

THREADS

Partly in response to the demand from machine embroiderers, the range of threads now offered by manufacturers has vastly increased in recent years and is being constantly added to.

Rayons come in a tremendous range of colours, including plain, shaded and multicolour. Madeira 40's Rayon has a very high tensile strength, whilst the Madeira 30's Rayon is thicker and more lustrous. Widely available is an Indian Natesh 30's thread which comes in a wide range of colours, both plain and multicoloured. It has the advantage of being comparatively cheap, which is a consideration when used in quantity, but it does lack a little in strength. Other threads include silks, cotton and metallics. A matt wool textured thread provides a contrast to all the shiny threads available. Shade cards are available by mail order to borrow or to buy. When you are buying thread for a particular project, it is better to buy the 1000 metre reels of thread as the smaller 200 metre reels get used very quickly. The dye lots can also vary from batch to batch. Use a matching or contrasting colour in a no. 30 or 50 machine embroidery thread in the bobbin, regardless of what you are using on the top.

For the actual construction and making up of cushions, quilts, etc use

There is an enormous range of threads available today in a wonderful range of colours.

an ordinary sewing thread, which has a higher twist than machine embroidery threads.

THE SEWING MACHINE

It is possible to do decorative stitching with a basic straight stitch machine, with the foot on and the feed dog up, but the potential is limited. You can vary the tension from tight to loose and the stitch length from short to long as shown on this page. Different threads and fabrics will make all the difference to the resulting stitch. Quilting and applying fabric are also possible.

A swing needle automatic machine is the next progression. As well as straight stitch, this will do zigzag stitch (see below, centre) and by altering the stitch to as near 0 as possible you get satin stitch (see below, right). These machines sometimes have a few built-in stitch patterns, altered by a lever or alternatively by inserting discs, known as 'cams', into the machine. Experiment with combina-

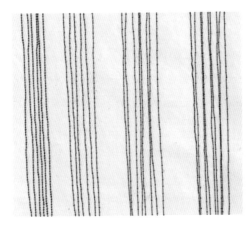

Straight stitch, from the shortest to the longest.

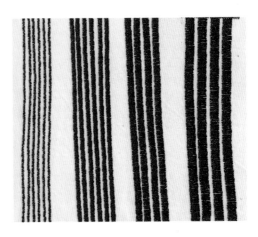

Satin stitch, from the narrowest to the widest.

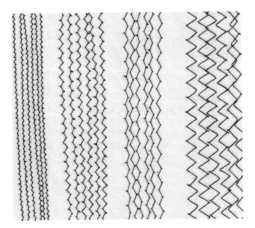

Zigzag stitch, from the shortest to the longest.

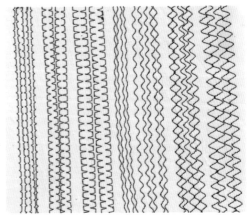

Machine stitch patterns

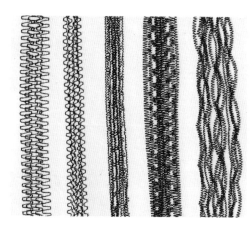

Overlapping and over-stitching the same machine stitch pattern.

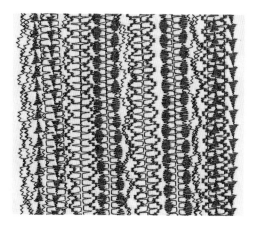

Combining and over-stitching different stitch patterns.

individual stitch variations. Even newer are machines where designs can be produced on a computer linked to the sewing machine and reproduced in stitch!

A wide variety of effects can be achieved on all these machines by using them with the feed dog up and the presser foot on. Variations are made by changing stitch length or tension, and by using the different feet and attachments that come with the machine: the buttonhole foot, tailor tacking foot, cording foot, gathering foot, braiding foot, pintuck foot, piping foot, ruffler. Some machines have an eyelet circular embroidery attachment; these might be a little too regular but could be personalised by overstitching or cutting fabric up into irregular shapes and restitching it on to another background.

A sampler of the variety of tones that can be achieved using light, open machine stitch patterns through to dense, dark patterns.

tions of the stitch patterns, by overlapping them and varying the stitch length or width.

Fully automatic machines do straight stitching, zigzag and a larger variety of stitch patterns. The sewing speed can be varied and the feed dog can be lowered by pushing a button or lever.

The latest sewing machines are the computerised models. In addition to all the above, they incorporate a 'memory' into which can be fed combinations of stitches to produce

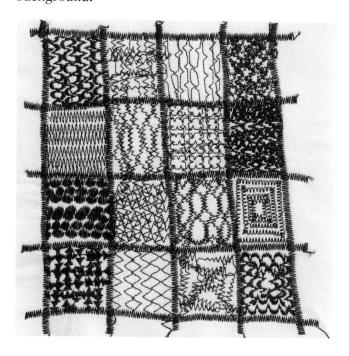

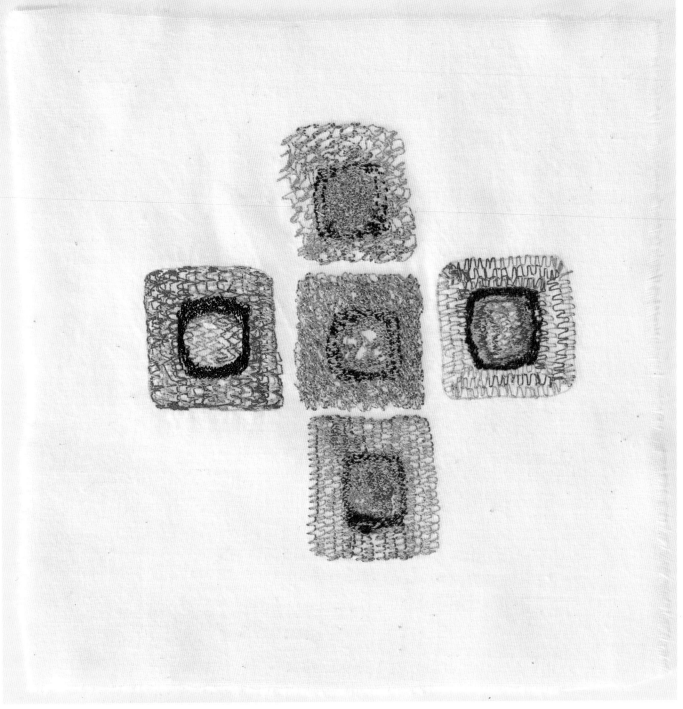

Free machine stitching – with the machine set to zigzag.

FREE MACHINE EMBROIDERY

This is where full reign can be given to the imagination, but it does take practice to develop confidence.

Consult the instruction booklet acquired with your sewing machine. If you find it is capable of darning, then it should be capable of free machining, i.e. the ability to move the fabric under the needle without restriction. Tightly framed fabric is used or a stiffened fabric which means you are not confined to stitching small areas at a time. For your practice samples use a medium-weight fabric, such as cotton, tightly framed, and a larger needle size, 90 or 100, as these break less easily than the finer ones.

Lower or cover the feed dog, according to the instruction manual, and use the darning foot supplied with the machine. It may help to reduce the top tension slightly, especially when using metallic threads. Set the machine for straight stitching and the stitch length to 0 (you now control the stitch length by moving the frame quickly or slowly). To make the sample more interesting, draw a very simple pattern on the fabric: circles, squares, triangles or combinations of these. Now try filling in the pattern with different doodles: side-to-side, vermicelli, cross hatching, circles, tiny squares, etc. Try another sample using the zigzag stitch.

Free machine stitching – straight stitched shapes filled in with various doodles, including circles, triangles and cross hatching.

Free machine stitching –
using various machine
stitch patterns.

Then try the various built-in patterns of the machine to see what effect they create. These patterns can be cut out and appliquéd on to projects, as on the bolster cushion on page 58.

Remember, you are aiming to achieve an individual piece of work. If there is a slight mis-alignment of pattern in your machine embroidery, then so much the better. Get to know your own sewing machine; do some samples and get used to working with it in a relaxed way. Combinations of automatic stitch patterns and free machining, together with the wonderful range of fabrics and threads available, will give you endless scope for invention.

CARE OF YOUR SEWING MACHINE

It is very important to keep the machine in good working order and this will save hours of frustration. The average domestic sewing machine used for dressmaking or the odd set of curtains does not run for hours at a time, which can happen with machine embroidery.

Make it a habit when finishing for the day to clean out the fluff and dirt from in and around the bobbin race and feed dogs – it's amazing how much collects there. Oil the bobbin case. A spot of sewing machine oil on the fingers, rubbed over the back of the bobbin case and around its edges, will reduce friction and wear and tear. The machine will run more quietly.

Decorative stitching and quilting can be done on your sewing machine.

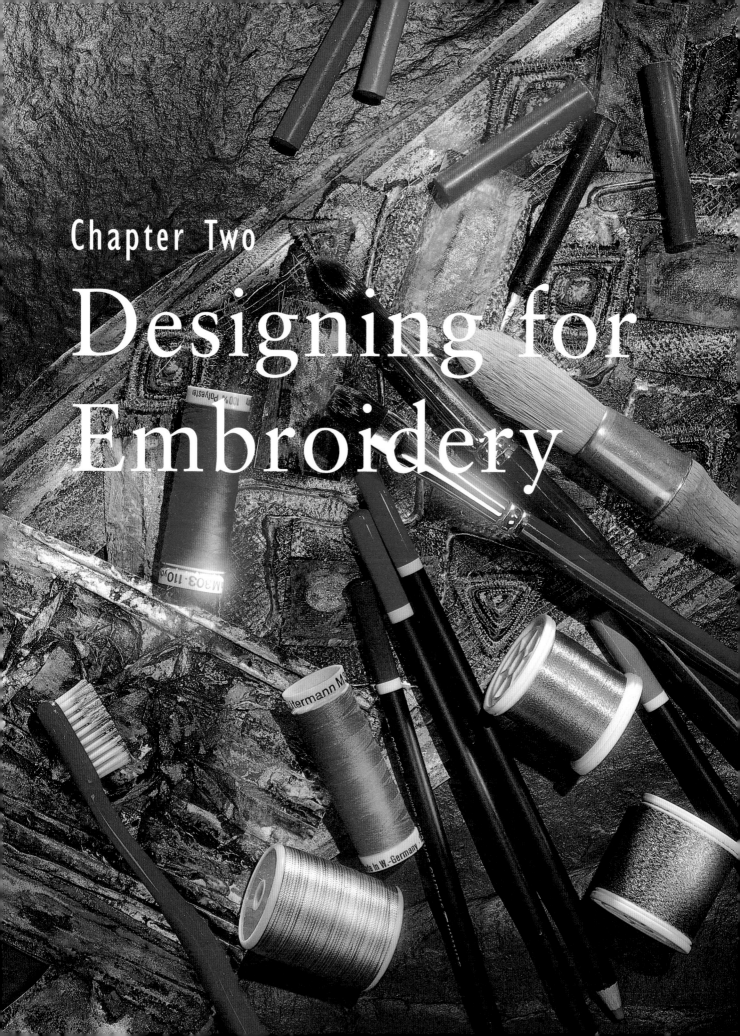

Chapter Two

Designing for Embroidery

Designing for Embroidery

Above: A selection of some of the different kinds of paper you can use for designing your embroideries.

Opposite: The textures of hand-made paper are inspiring. Here a selection is shown using the techniques described.

The basic materials for design start very simply with something to draw on – paper – and something to draw or paint with – pencils, pens, paintbrushes, crayons, pastels, inks and paints. Put your ideas down on to paper, and then translate into fabric and thread.

PAPER

Collect as many different types of paper as you can find, including tissue, card, corrugated paper, lining paper, brown paper, paper bags, napkins, kitchen roll, photocopy paper, crêpe paper. All these will have different properties which give various textural results and could lead to different interpretations in your use of fabric, thread and techniques.

There are specialist paper shops. These stock a wide range of beautiful papers: handmade, Japanese, lace, textured vegetable fibre, leather-like. The list is endless. Your own handmade paper is especially nice to use as it has a different feel to any paper you can buy. It is more textured and you can control how thick or thin it is; you can also control the size of each sheet. Various things can be added to it at the pulp stage – seeds, leaves and small scraps of fabric and/or thread. There are many specialist books about papermaking. However, the following is a simple recipe for handmade paper.

HANDMADE PAPER RECIPE

Most paper is recyclable into handmade paper – anything, in fact, that doesn't have a shiny surface. It is also best to avoid heavily printed newspaper, which might be too obvious in the finished result. Computer paper,

1. Tear your selected paper into tiny scraps.

2. Leave to soak overnight in a bowl or a bucket, to break down the fibres, or if you are in a hurry boil it for an hour or so.

3. The next stage will vary according to the size of liquidizer you use. Put a small amount of the prepared scraps into the liquidizer and add 0.5 litre of cold water. Do not over-liquidize the paper – you want it to look hand-made and textured.

4. Put the resulting paper pulp into a bowl or tray (garden or cat litter trays are ideal). Add more water until the tray is about half full. Stir the mixture to suspend the paper pulp.

5. Take a piece of net, canvas or scrim. Holding it tautly, dip it sharply into the tray; a layer of pulp will be deposited on the surface. Drain off the excess water and leave the sheet of paper to dry. If you want to make plain sheets of paper, the simplest method is to make a mould from a small picture frame, tacked with net. Follow steps 1-5 as above, then continue.

6. Place a wad of newspapers on a table with an all-purpose kitchen cloth on top.

7. After dipping the flat side of the net-covered frame into the pulp mixture, allow the water to drain off and the pulp to settle, then turn the mould, paper side down, onto the cloth. Lift the mould carefully off the resulting sheet of paper. (It may help to press down with a sponge into the well of the frame to ease away the paper).

8. Place another cloth over the sheet of paper.

9. Add more newspapers and another cloth and repeat the process as many times as you want.

VARIATIONS

1. Use plastic canvas as a mould – this produces regular squares of varying sizes.

2. Use ordinary sewing canvas.

3. Wrap threads fairly closely around a wooden frame and use this as a mould.

brown paper bags, envelopes, letters, photocopier paper, paper napkins and tissue paper. Even coloured papers are useful as you can start with these as the base colour.

PENS, PENCILS, CRAYONS, PAINTS, INKS

The wider the range of drawing materials you use, the more varied your designs will be. If you continually work in one particular medium, all your designs are going to be very similar and somewhat lacking in interest.

Start with a small collection of crayons, oil pastels and primary colours of ink, gold and silver paints or crayons and acrylic paints. Combine media, using inks with wax crayons, acrylics with oil pastels. The different media combined with various papers will give endless combinations for your designs. Each experiment will reveal different results and textures, which in turn will suggest what fabrics and threads to use in your final embroidery.

A few other products which you might find useful for designing are gesso, texture paste, household emulsion, varnish, bleach, gold leaf or bronze powder.

BRUSHES

All kinds of brushes are worth experimenting with: paintbrushes (household), round-ended and flat-ended brushes, fan-shaped brushes, stencil brushes with stiff bristles, old-toothbrushes, make-up brushes, even the brushes that come with kits for perming your hair!

DESIGN TECHNIQUES

The very word 'design' throws most people into a panic but really it is very simple. It means sorting out the ideas in your mind into some kind of order before translating them into fabric and thread. You can then make a decision based on the result and decide which idea you are going to work your embroidery from. If you dive straight into stitching with the first idea you have, it tends to be a little hit-or-miss. You could waste precious materials and even more precious time.

By designing on paper first you give yourself a number of options to choose from. Your first idea is not usually the best; it needs to be worked at. You may reach a stage when nothing seems to be going right and you almost give up, but this frequently turns out to be the best design of all.

How often have you drawn a little doodle with a pen or pencil whilst talking on the telephone – filled it in, drawn little repeats of it, filled in the shapes with patterns? It's amazing what you can do with just one simple shape; initially don't go to great expense by buying vast ranges of colours in every medium possible. You only need the primary colours red, yellow and blue, as from these all the other colours can be mixed. There are some excellent books on the subject of colour and colour mixing; you can usually borrow some from your local library.

Later in this book designs and instructions are given for various projects. These will also encourage you to try your own designing on paper and then translate the designs into cushions, wallhangings and other home furnishings.

The following techniques are just a few of the many ways of designing. The first are design sources in themselves. The resulting designs used on their own, or in conjunction with other design techniques, will enable you to create very different and personal effects. It's not difficult, and it is very satisfying.

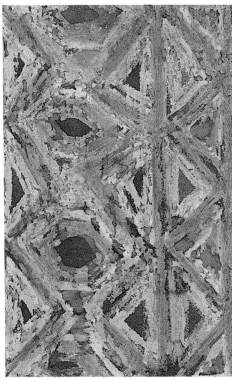

Stage 1 Take a sheet of white paper and ordinary wax crayons. Draw a shape or shapes – close together, spaced out, overlapped. Draw smaller versions within the larger shapes.

Stage 2 Pour some black writing ink diluted with a little water, into a dish. Take a paintbrush and cover the entire sheet of paper with ink. The ink will cover any paper left uncovered by the wax, but not the wax crayon drawing.

Stage 3 & 4 When the ink has dried, draw on top using oil pastels (bottom left) or a gold fine liner pen (bottom right).

What you have just produced is a wax crayon resist design. Easy, isn't it – and very effective.

Gouache and liquid acrylic on black paper.

BLOT PAINTINGS

This is an unpredictable technique but the results are often very beautiful.

1. Fold a sheet of paper in half and open it out again.

2. Use watered-down acrylic paints or metallic gouache and pearlescent liquid acrylics. Drop blobs of paint down the centre of the paper, on the fold or near to it. Do not fill more than half the sheet of paper with paint as it has a habit of oozing out of the sides if you use too much.

3. Carefully refold the sheet of paper, pushing from the centre fold outward towards the edges.

4. Open out the paper again, pulling it apart gently. You should now have a lovely random design. Experiment with blot paintings on black paper using metallic gouache and, using black pen, draw on your designs when they are dry.

Liquid acrylic with black pen design.

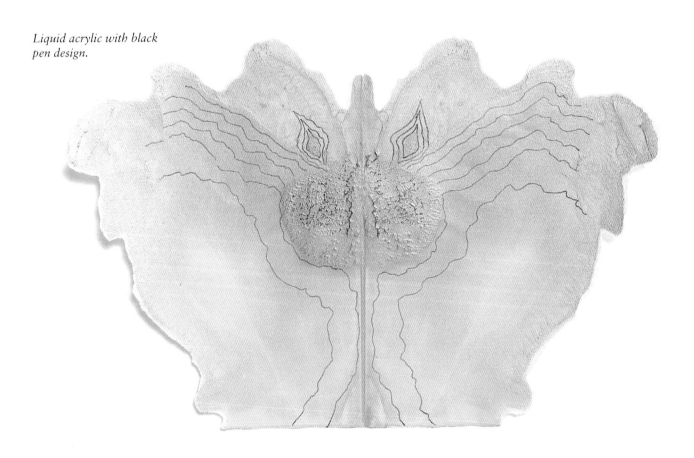

*Coloured tissue paper
cut into shapes and glued
to white paper. It is
rubbed with gold and
silver paints when dry.*

DESIGNING WITH TISSUE PAPER

This is another very simple, effective way of random designing.

1. Collect as many different colours of tissue paper as you can find. You need very little in each colour. Crumple the tissue paper up in your hands and tear it into pieces.

2. Glue the pieces of tissue to a base layer of white paper, using PVA glue. It helps to thin the PVA down a little with water. Cover the whole of the sheet of white paper with PVA then start applying the tissue, pasting over the top of each colour in places. Crumple the tissue even more as you glue it down. Overlap the pieces so that other subdued colours appear. When you have completely covered the surface of the white paper, leave it to dry.

3. When dry, rub gold or silver acrylic paint over the surface of the tissue (see above). If you want a more organized pattern, cut the tissue into shapes and glue down as above, repeating the process.

   I like using these designs as frames for small embroideries. You could also develop embroideries from them by using layers of coloured organzas stitched with metal thread.

SCRIBBLE DESIGNS

Scribble drawing using wax crayons. The drawing is then washed over with black writing ink.

1. Using a pencil, scribble randomly over a sheet of paper, making circles and crossing over previously drawn lines until you are pleased with the shapes.

2. Fill in the drawings with wax crayons or paint your design with acrylic colours, rather like filling in a child's colouring book. If you used wax crayons, paint your design with a wash of black ink as shown here.

These designs could also be used for patchwork, quilting or free machine embroidery.

CUT AND TORN PAPER DESIGNS

This can be a most effective source of designing.

1. Build up your design on a background sheet of paper. It can consist of very simple shapes: squares, diamonds, triangles, etc. Tear some of the shapes and cut others; notice the difference between the two. Alter the scale, making some large and some small. Use different types of paper (tissue, cartridge, hand-made) to give a contrast of textures.

2. Arrange the design on the background sheet of paper. When you are pleased with the result, glue it down and leave it to dry.

3. At this stage there are a number of materials you can use to achieve different effects:

(a) Lay a wash on your design using coloured inks. Leave to dry and colour with oil pastels rubbed over with acrylic paint (undiluted). Glue paper shapes on top.

(b) Paint a wash of ink over the paper design – brown or black works well. Pour a little thick domestic bleach into a dish and paint either the whole design or just parts of it with the bleach solution. Do use old brushes for this, not your best ones, and rinse your brushes thoroughly immediately after use. Take great care not to splash yourself with the bleach. The bleach will alter the ink's surface considerably so do a little at a time until you are satisfied with the result. Black ink bleached out produces yellow browns and cream: brown ink bleached out gives greenish tinges and cream. When the ink and bleach are dry you can draw on top of the design, using oil pastels, etc.

(c) Print on to your design, using a sponge or potato and metallic acrylics, then paint over this.

(d) Combine these different methods by cutting or tearing sections out and placing them over another design.

Torn strips of dimpled packaging paper and kitchen roll are glued to a white cartridge base. Cut geometric shapes are then glued on top. The design is washed with purple and turquoise ink and rubbed over with gold paint when dry. Star shapes are cut from another design, placed on top and stitched in place.

Torn strips of hand-made paper are applied to a white cartridge paper base. Cut geometric shapes are glued on top and washed with brown writing ink. Thick bleach is applied, giving a greenish tinge. An application of colour is given with oil pastels and a wash of red drawing ink.

The base is a chequer-board pattern of pre-painted brown paper bag squares. Textured paper shapes are glued on top and decorated with oil pastels. These are then washed with turquoise and red ink. The top layer is made up of tissue paper shapes which are applied over a grid of paper ribbon. Gold paint is sponged on and turquoise and black ink washed over. When the paper is dry, gold paint is rubbed in and the design is then machine zigzag stitched.

Right: Potato printed triangles in blue acrylic are overpainted with acrylic gold paint. The shapes are filled in with red ink and the whole design is washed with diluted turquoise ink.

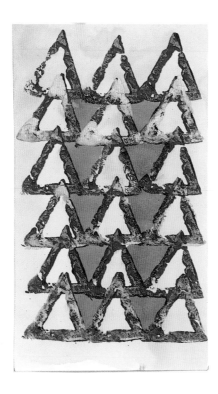

Below left: Potato printed shapes using gold paint on black paper, drawn over with coloured crayons. Right: potato printed shapes using gold paint on black paper, drawn over with oil pastels.

POTATO AND SPONGE PRINTING

1. Cut a potato in half and carve simple shapes on the exposed surfaces, trimming away the sides to leave a raised design. Blot the cut surface of the potato with kitchen roll.

2. Mix the paint in a flattish dish or plate. Press the potato design on to the paint or, preferably, use a brush to load the paint on to the potato.

3. Lay the fabric on a layer of white paper on a completely flat surface. Position the potato carefully and print the shape, pressing down hard. Reload the potato with paint each time for a regular amount of colour or alternatively use it to print more than once, which will leave less colour with each impression.

The illustration opposite shows potato prints in gold acrylic on black cotton fabric, stitched in various ways.

Sponges can be cut to shape with scissors. They are best loaded by being pressed into the paint and, like potatoes, they can be used for more than one repeat, each getting paler and paler.

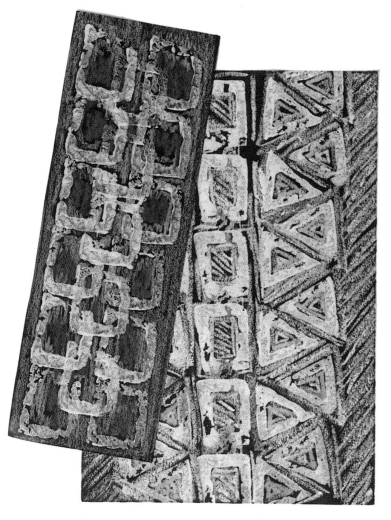

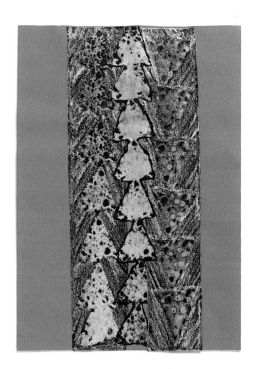

A sponge design printed in light gold gouache. Oil pastels are used to draw around the design.

Basic potato print in gold gouache on fabric.
Variations (left to right) satin stitch and machine
stitched pattern in multicoloured rayon thread;
random-dyed leather applied with zigzag stitch
with a straight pattern overlaid; machine stitched
patterns on black net appliquéd to the centres of
the shapes; quilted design in narrow zigzag stitch.

Left: Lino print in black acrylic on pre-painted background of fan-brushed red and yellow inks.

Below: Lino print in gold acrylic on black tissue paper, drawn on to with oil pastels. The design of a star is translated into fabric and thread. The star is satin stitched in multicoloured thread on scrim.

LINO PRINTING

Although slightly more complicated than any of the previous methods, lino printing has the advantage of allowing you to draw very fine designs with good detail into a lino block. This makes it much less child-like than any of the other simple printing techniques. Lino blocks and lino-carving tools are normally available at any good art suppliers.

Use simple shapes for your designs to begin with, just to get the feel of it. Then, if you like the technique, work out a series of squares and triangles with a different pattern in each.

1. Draw your design on to a lino tile in pencil first, then carve it out using the various gouges. Take great care to push the carving tools away from you, as they are extremely sharp!

2. Use sheets of ready-prepared paper, hand-made or commercial, left plain or pre-painted by rolling with different coloured inks, paints, gold and acrylics, etc, or maybe sponged or marbled. Place a sheet of paper on a wad of newspaper.

3. Take a piece of glass (tape the edges first to avoid cut fingers!) and squeeze black acrylic paint on to it. Spread with a brush, just enough to cover the area of the lino block.

4. Place the lino block, carved side down, on the acrylic paint. Using a small handroller, roll over the back of the block in all directions so that the paint is transferred to the raised portions of the lino block.

5. Peel off the lino block from the glass and place in position on the paper. Again using the handroller, roll the back of the block in all directions, pressing firmly to ensure that the whole design is transferred to the paper.

6. Peel off the lino block carefully and re-position it to repeat the pattern.

You can, of course, use different coloured acrylic paints to print with. You could overprint the pattern by offsetting it slightly or overprint in different colours, for example, pearlescent shades over black.

These are just a few of the ways of achieving different designs. You can use any of the techniques in this chapter on their own, or you can mix them. The results will be stunning and you will have created your own unique design.

PRINTING WITH POLYSTYRENE

If you have access to a soldering iron, you can easily make printing blocks from polystyrene tiles or the polystyrene food trays you get from supermarkets.

1. Work out your design on paper then draw it on the polystyrene, using a biro.

2. Heat the soldering iron. Following the instructions carefully, run the tip of the soldering iron over the polystyrene, following the outlines of your design. Be careful not to burn right through the polystyrene.

3. Follow the directions opposite for lino printing. Polystyrene printing blocks are quick to make and seem to produce endless prints without wearing out. They produce very free images.

Two designs using polystyrene block prints and a gold acrylic which are washed with blue and red drawing inks.

Chapter Three
Square & Rectangular Cushions

Square & Rectangular Cushions

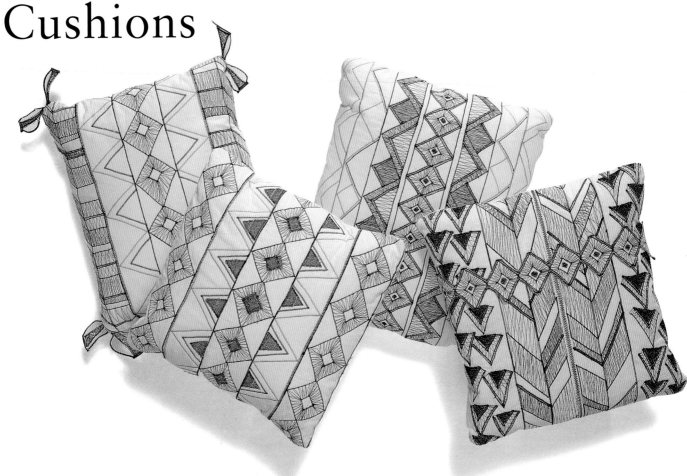

The Elizabethans loved the contrast between black and white. This theme is carried through in the set of four cushions (above and in more detail on pages 42-43). Calico, with a cream felt backing, is free-machine stitched using a variety of zigzag and straight stitches to create lines and tones.

STUFFINGS AND FILLINGS

It is easier to buy inner pads for cushions ready made, rather than having to make them yourself. Filling cushions with feathers must be done outside on a windless day and, of course, there is the problem of where to get the feathers from in the first place. For those who are allergic to feathers, there are polyester fibre-filled cushion pads, which are soft as well as being washable. The only cushion pads not recommended are those filled with foam chippings, which feel cheap and are not comfortable. The aim is firm, plump cushions which feel luxurious and inviting to sink down into.

CUSHION SIZES

Standard square cushions come in a range of sizes, the commonest being 38 x 38 cm (15 x 15 in) and 46 x 46 cm (18 x 18 in) which gives a more opulent look. The haberdashery or soft furnishing section of your local department store will stock the basic sizes and they can often be bought in pairs at a slightly cheaper price. Larger stores in cities usually stock a much wider range of cushion pads in different sizes and shapes.

MAKING UP CUSHION COVERS

There are various methods of making up your finished embroidery into a cushion cover.

The simplest is to machine stitch round three sides of the front and back cover; right sides together. To prevent the cushion having pointed corners, pin approximately 3 cm (1 in) in on either side of each corner and tack a curve between the pinned points (Fig. 1). Turn the cover to the right side, press the seams, insert the cushion pad and slipstitch the fourth side by hand.

However, if the cushion needs to be washed regularly it will be a nuisance to have to re-stitch the seam each time.

CUSHION WITH ZIPS

Place the front and back cover right sides together. Machine stitch 5 cm (2 in) from either end of one side as shown in Fig. 2. Insert the zip in the opening and stitch in place (Fig. 3). Press the seams. Stitch the remaining three sides, clip the corners and press. Turn to the right side, leaving the zip slightly open.

If the embroidery is bulky (eg. heavily quilted or very dense machine stitching) and it would be difficult to insert the zip on the edge, move it to the centre back (Fig. 4, page 40) or to one side (Fig. 5).

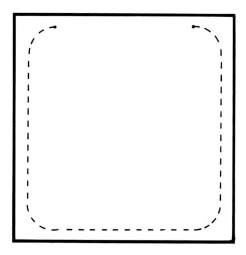

Figure 1: Stitch a curve at each corner of the cushion.

Figure 2: Stitch 5 cm (2 in) from either end.

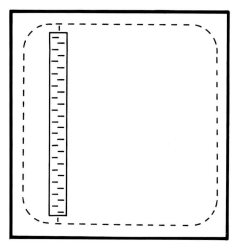

Figure 3: Insert the zip in the opening.

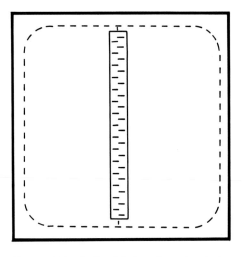

Figure 4: For bulky fabrics, place the zip in the centre back of the cushion.

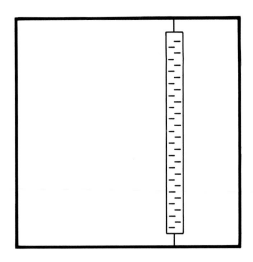

Figure 5: Alternatively, position the zip on one side of the back cushion.

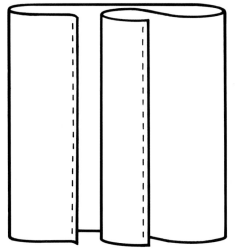

Figure 6: Turn under the edges of the cushion cover and stitch.

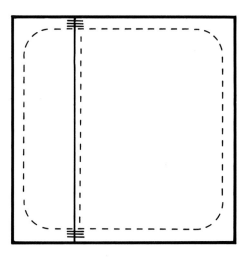

Figure 7: Do a few reverse stitches to strengthen where the seam overlaps.

CUSHION WITH PLACKETS

For those of you who dislike inserting zips, an envelope placket could be the answer, although it does use more fabric.

Cut out the back of the cushion cover into pieces, allowing a seam allowance of 1.5cm (¹/₂ in) plus an additional 25 cm (10 in) overlap. Turn under the raw edges on the back cover as shown in Fig. 6. Stitch and press flat. With right sides together, stitch all four sides of the cover. To give extra strength where the seam overlaps, sew a few stitches in reverse and then carry on (Fig. 7). This treble-stitches the seam where it takes the strain of removing the cushion pads and putting them back. Clip the corners, turn the cover to the right side and press.

VARIATIONS ON A THEME

If you are making a set of co-ordinated cushions do little sketches or doodles of the design in the cushion shapes, varying the position of the design on each one. This way your cushions will go well together without being sets of strict repeats.

Using the same techniques or colours throughout will give visual impact. Try using the same colours while varying the technique, or use the same technique but vary the colours.

Sketches of possible co-ordinating designs.

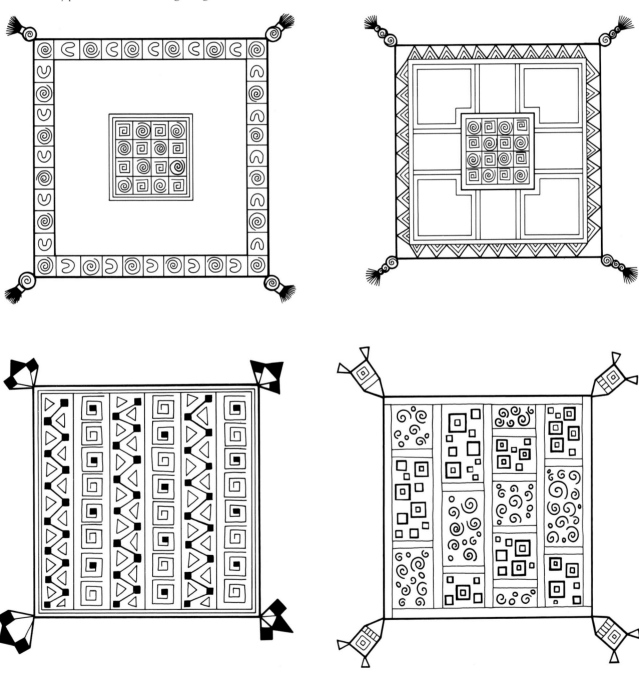

ELIZABETHAN BLACK AND WHITE CUSHIONS

The contrast between black and white is dramatic and satisfying, and as popular today as it was in Tudor days.

The set of cushions on the previous page is based on the Elizabethans' much-loved contrast of black on white. Various samples were stitched before deciding on the final designs below.

METHOD

You will need 4 cushion pads 38 x 38 cm (15 x 15 in) and enough fabric to cover them. Calico and cream felt are used on the front of the covers and calico on the backs, which are finished with envelope plackets (see page 40).

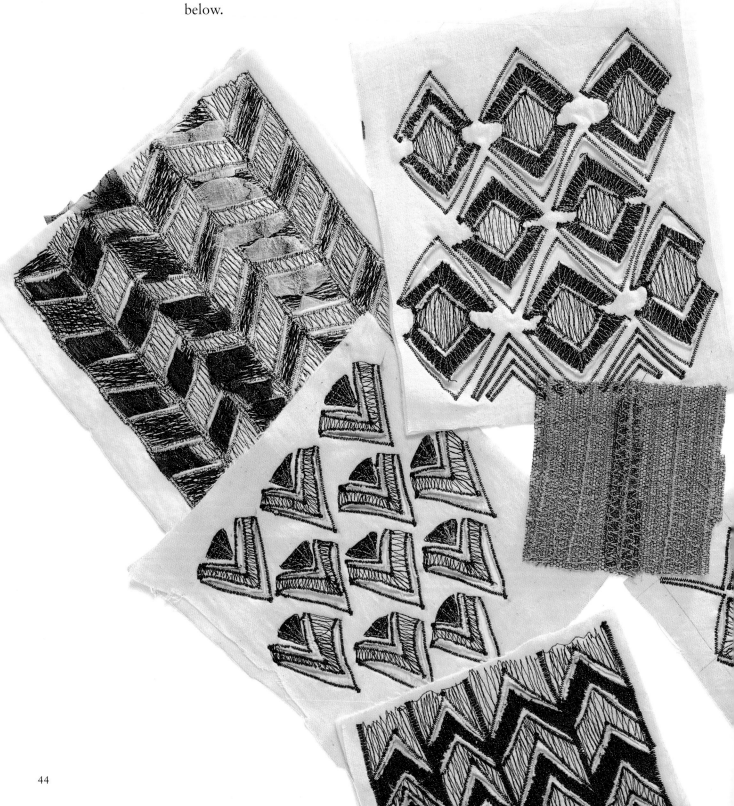

A 40.5 cm (16 in) square of calico is placed on top of a square of felt of the same size, and the designs free-machined over the whole surface. Some metal thread is introduced and machine-stitched net is appliquéd to one of the cushions to highlight and vary the design. Double calico would be just as effective as the calico and felt. The reason for using this fabric is that it enables you to do free machine-stitching without the aid of a hoop. When you cut out the fabric to the size of the cushion pad, add an extra 3 cm (1 ¼ in) to allow for any shrinkage with the stitching, plus a seam allowance of 1.5 cm (½ in).

Using a narrow zigzag stitch with the feed dogs up and the presser foot on, stitch the background lines first, as shown in Fig. 9. Draw diamond and triangle shapes on top of this and stitch again with the same zigzag stitch (Fig. 10). When the basic outlines are completed replace the presser foot with a darning foot and lower the feeding dogs. Fill in parts of the design with free machining, creating different tonal areas by stitching more heavily in some areas than others (Fig. 11). Make up the cushion as described on page 39.

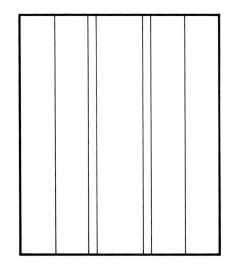

Figure 9: Stitch the background lines first.

Figure 10: Draw diamond and triangle shapes, then zigzag stitch.

Figure 11: Fill in the design with free machining.

BLACK QUILTED AND APPLIQUÉ CUSHION

A turtle shell inspired the design on the cushion shown here. The basic design is printed on to black fabric using a potato printing method. More colours are painted on, then layers of fabric are machine quilted together using metallic threads. The appliqué centres are made by stitching black organza to the fabric using a wide zigzag setting.

This design originated from a drawing of the patterns on a turtle shell (Fig. 12) and was subsequently translated into a paper design. The simple potato printing method is used to transfer the design on to the fabric.

METHOD

Allow enough fabric to cover the cushion pad. Here I used a 38 x 38 cm (15 x 15 in) cushion pad and black cotton fabric. Add 3 cm (1 1/4 in) to allow for any shrinkage caused by the machine stitching and a 1.5 cm (1/2 in) seam allowance.

Using the turtle shell drawing shown here trace off one of the large shapes and carve it on to a potato (see page 32). To print the design on to the black fabric with gold acrylic: pour the undiluted acrylic paint into a dish, blot the potato before using it for the first time, then apply the gold acrylic to the potato with a brush and print. Repeat as many times as you need to cover the cushion. Once you have printed all the basic shapes, overpaint them in a different colour using a pearlized acrylic paint. To quilt the design, use polyester wadding and a fine cotton backing fabric. Sandwich the three layers together, with the black printed fabric on top, and baste. Machine quilt around the shapes, using a metallic thread and with the sewing machine set for a fine zigzag, with the feed dogs up and the presser foot on. Using a machine stitch pattern and a different thread, quilt between the shapes.

The appliqué centres were made by stitching black organza with a metallic thread, using a wide zigzag set almost to satin stitch, but not quite. Between these stitched lines machine patterning was again used, overstitching frequently as this has to be cut into shapes to fill the centres (below left). Remember to use a metal thread in the bobbin as well as the top thread as it will show through and you may prefer the reverse side. Again following the original drawing (top left), cut out shapes to fill the centres of the printed pattern and machine in place with zigzag stitch.

Save all the little scraps of organza that you cut off – you can make another fabric with these by using hot water dissolve (below right) and this can be used for another project or for reference.

Make up the cushion using one of the methods described (see page 39).

Finish with piping, using satin bias binding.

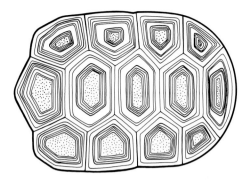

Figure 12: This drawing of the patterns on a turtle's shell inspired the design for the appliquéd cushion.

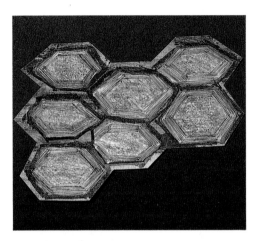

A coloured paper design of the turtle shell sketch.

VARIATIONS

1. Print the shapes onto the fabric in an organized pattern or entirely randomly. Overlap the shapes if you wish.

2. Use a straight stitch when quilting.

3. Use a multicoloured thread.

4. Use net instead of organza for the appliqué centres.

5. Use the hot water dissolve fabric below to fill some of the centres.

Left: Zigzag stitching in metallic thread on black organza.

Far left: Left-over fabric trapped between two layers of hot water dissolvable fabric and stitched with metallic thread.

Figure 13: Star design to trace off the page.

Figure 14: Alternative star design to trace off the page.

SMALL STAR CUTWORK CUSHION

Metallic threads and gold paint add a sparkle to this star-spangled design which reveals a layer of brightly coloured organza beneath the top fabric.

You will need white cotton fabric and coloured organza. Trace one of the star designs in Figs. 13 and 14 and transfer to a lino tile. Carve as described on page 34. Using gold acrylic paint, print the design onto white cotton fabric already cut to the size you wish to cover. Here, a small cushion pad is used, 30.5 x 30.5 cm (12 x 12 in). Add 3 cm (1 in) to allow for any shrinkage and 1.5cm (^{1}/$_2$ in) seam allowance. Repeat the design as many times as it is necessary to cover the whole cushion front.

Using metallic threads and satin stitch, machine stitch around as many of the star shapes as you wish. Complete the outline of these shapes, then cut away the star centres.

Place a layer of coloured organza underneath the cushion front and re-stitch around the larger star shapes to hold them in place. This can be done in different-coloured threads, multi-coloured thread, or again using metallic threads.

To make the frill, measure the circumference of the cushion all the way around, then double it. As this is only a small cushion, a 3 cm (1^1/$_4$ in) frill is deep enough, so I allowed a width of 8 cm (3 in) for the gathering and seam allowance. Join the frill so that you have a continuous strip, then gather the fabric by working two rows of running stitch all the way round. Pin the frill to the cushion front, adjust the gathers and tack in position. Place the back and front cushion cover right sides together, tack and machine stitch. Turn to the right side and finish with a zip or placket (see page 39).

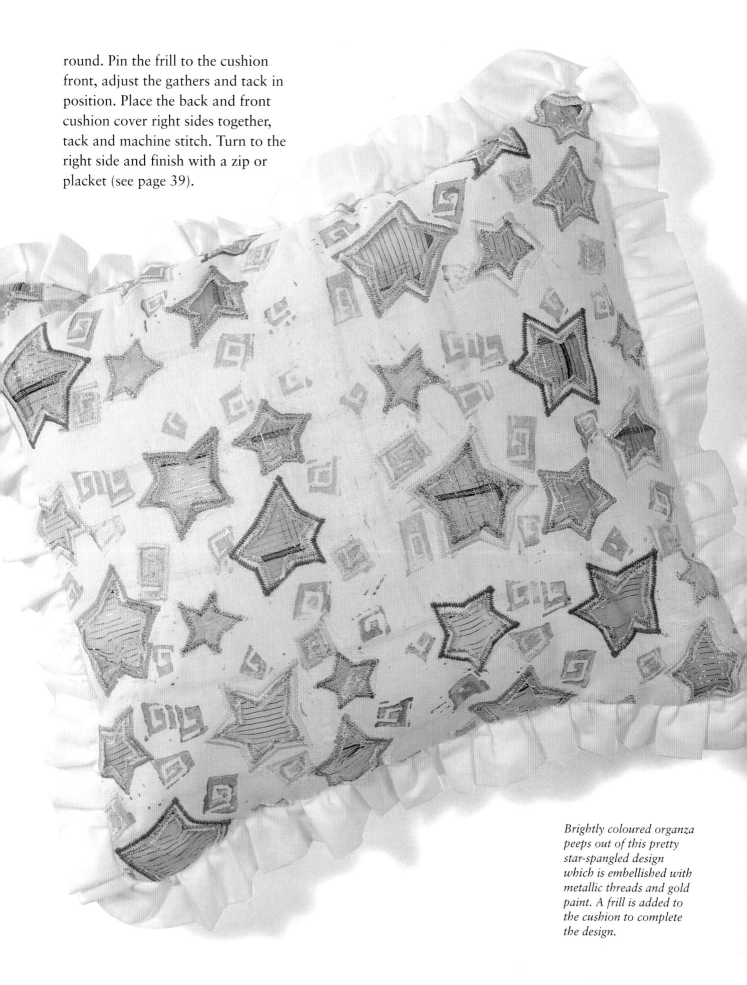

Brightly coloured organza peeps out of this pretty star-spangled design which is embellished with metallic threads and gold paint. A frill is added to the cushion to complete the design.

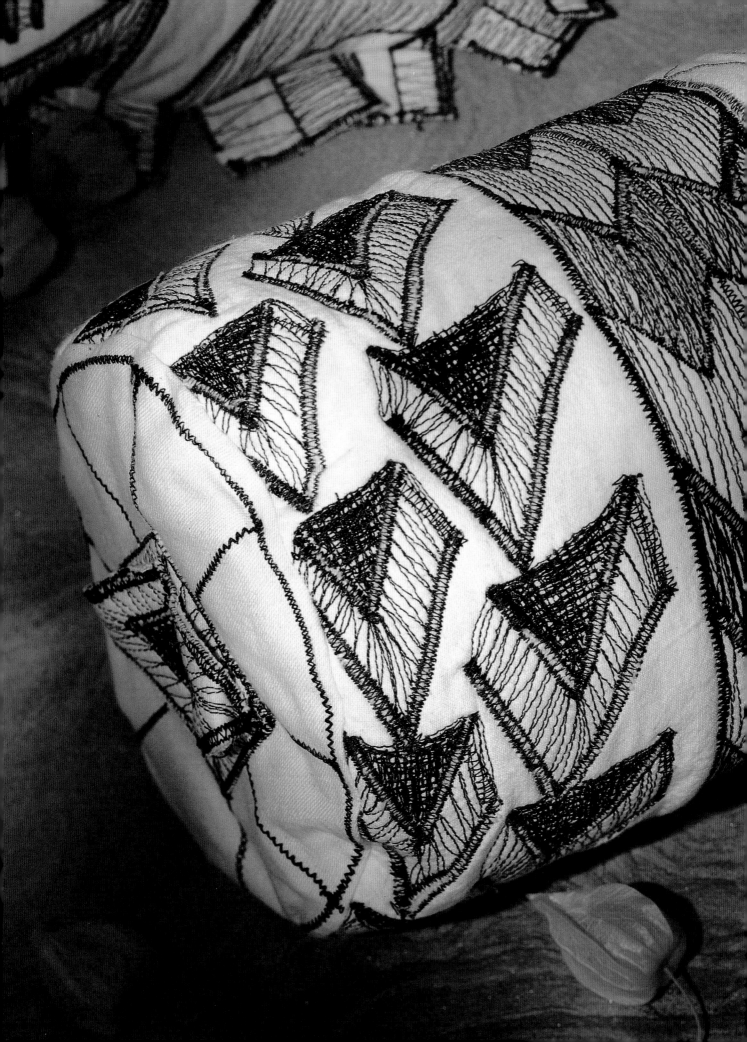

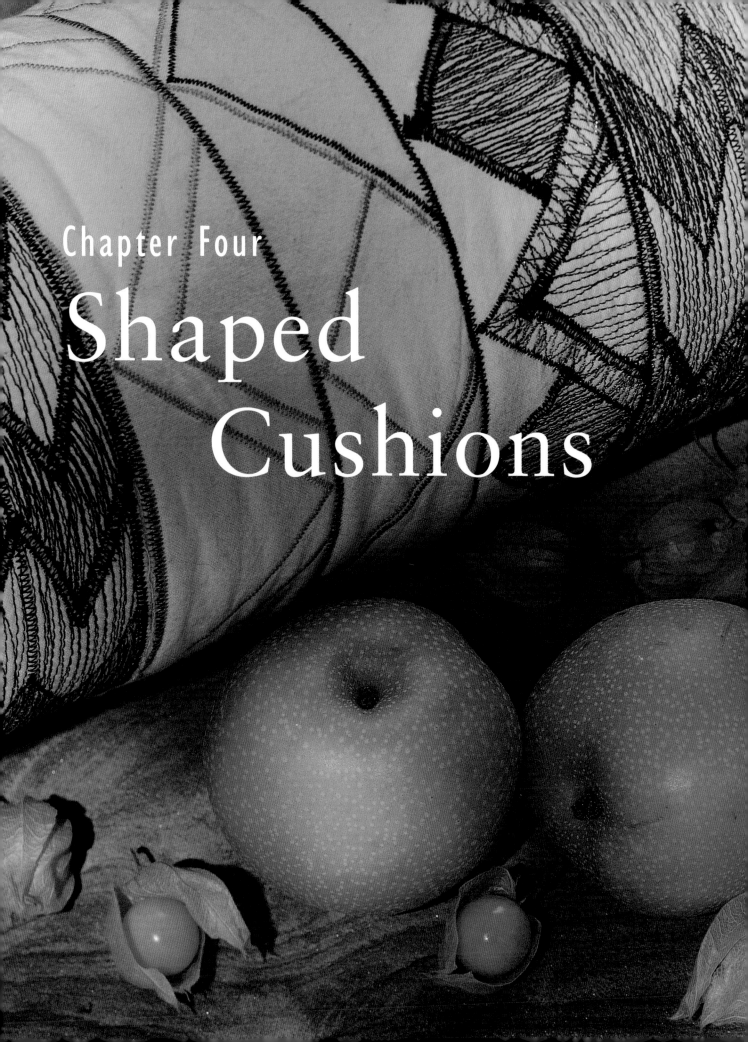

Chapter Four

Shaped
Cushions

Shaped Cushions

The only limitation I can see to shaped cushions is the ability to get the cushion pad in and out! Round ones (reasonably easy to buy), heart-shaped, triangular, fan-shaped, bolsters, fruit and vegetable shapes, shell shapes (based on the drawings on page 55) – anything goes.

If you cannot find the right cushion pad, improvise. Buy pillows and make your own shapes by pushing back the filling, pinning and then stitching it into the shape you want. Fig. 15 shows how to divide a pillow into three or four triangular cushions.

Bolster cushion pads are not easy to find either, so make your own. Roll up an ordinary square cushion, pin along the edges and oversew by hand twice, with a strong thread such as button thread.

Figure 15: How to make three or four triangular cushions from one pillow.

QUILTED STAR CUSHION

Trapunto and Italian quilting decorate this brightly coloured cushion, which is painted with dyes and embellished with black net. This cushion was designed to fit a 39 cm (15 in) round cushion pad.

METHOD
Draw around a circular cushion pad on brown paper to make a pattern. Fold into quarters and use a compass to check that it is completely round.

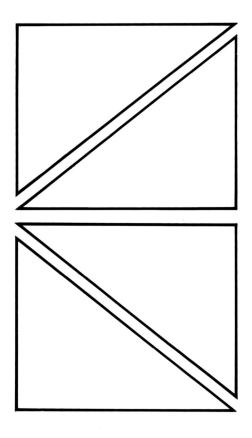

Cut out the front of the cushion in heavyweight calico, adding a seam allowance of 1 cm (¹/₂ in). Fold the paper pattern in half and cut two back sections, adding 1.5cm (¹/₂ in) on the curved sections and 2.5 cm (1 in) on the straight edges to allow for inserting the zip.

Fold the front cushion in quarters to find the centre, press lightly and open out. Two layers are needed for the techniques of trapunto and Italian

quilting so you will need to cut another circle in muslin or open-weave cotton. Using the creased lines on the calico as a guide, baste the calico and muslin together at 5 cm (2 in) intervals over the whole of the cushion front, in both directions. Scale up the star design (overleaf) to the size you need on graph paper or, better still, enlarge it on a photocopier. Trace the star design on to the muslin side of the cushion cover so

Metallic threads and gold paint add a sparkle to this small star-spangled design which reveals a layer of organza beneath the top fabric.

Scale up the star design to fit your cushion.

ITALIAN QUILTING

Thread a bodkin with quilting wool (available from most good needle-work suppliers) or cord, using it double if necessary. Working from the back of the cushion cover, make a hole with the bodkin through the muslin into the channels of double stitching. Occasionally it may be necessary at the point of the stars to pull the needle out and re-insert it, either in the same hole or a little further on.

FINISHING TOUCHES

Fill in the large space between the two outer stars by applying net, muslin or organza, stitched in place with a machine-stitched pattern. Work extra rows of machine-stitched patterns, in either black or a metallic thread.

When all the stuffing and stitching is completed you can paint the cushions with dyes or acrylic paints. It helps the colours to merge and blend if you first wet the calico and continue to add brushfuls of water if they are still not blending well. Gold acrylic paint helps to highlight certain areas. Make sure that you dye or paint the back of the cushion at the same time to get the same colours as the front. If you are using silk paints, heat–set them by ironing; acrylic paints should be left to 'cure' for 72 hours. Stitch a couple of beads in the centre of the trapunto star for extra decoration.

Insert a zip in the back of the cushion (page 39). With right sides together, stitch the back and front together – remember to leave the zip slightly open. Trim the seams, turn the cover to the right side and press.

that the lines will not show on the front of the cushion. Machine stitch the shapes in white or cream thread – one row of stitching for the central star (trapunto) and a double row for the two outer star shapes (Italian quilting) to make a channel to thread the quilting cord or wool through. When all the stitching lines are completed, withdraw the basting threads.

TRAPUNTO

Starting with the central star, cut a small slit in the muslin. Using polyester wadding or fleece and a crochet hook, push the filling out into the points of the star, working inwards towards the centre so that the star is padded and raised from the background. Oversew the slit with a few stitches to be secure.

*Inspiration and design:
an example of how
natural forms can be
turned into round
cushion shapes.*

ROUND BOW CUSHION

Machine whipstitch is used to draw the bows and background patterns. Small bows are worked separately and appliquéd on top of some of the stitched bows.

This was designed to fit a 30 cm (12 in) diameter round cushion pad. First mount a double layer of black fabric in an embroidery hoop or frame of that size, making sure to stretch the fabric taut. Cut out the material to the required size, using the method for the star cushion as I have described on page 52.

The embroidery is worked in machine whip stitch, in which the bobbin thread is brought up through the fabric to cover the top thread. Multi-coloured thread will save a lot of time changing bobbins; you have no control over the colours so just use a multi-coloured or shaded thread to start with. To get maximum effect from the colour of the bobbin thread, use an invisible thread on top –

as well as clear invisible thread, there is also a smoky grey for dark fabrics.

Set the machine to stitch length 0 and width 0, with the top tension tight and the bobbin tension normal or slightly loose (turn the small tension screw in the bobbin case). Remove the pressure foot; if you dislike machining without a foot use the darning foot.

Working in the well of the embroidery hoop or frame, use the machine needle like a pen to draw bow shapes, following the direction of the arrows in Fig. 18. For the central knot of each bow, work small rectangles or circles. Stitch as many bows as you need to fill the embroidery hoop or frame. When you have practised with a few you can vary the rest, making them fat or thin, large or small, curved or straight. To get from one bow to the next, don't take the needle out of the fabric but simply move the needle, filling in the background as you go with worm-like doodles. If you feel really adventurous you could stitch tiny flowers in the background spaces.

Once you have outlined all the bow shapes you need, go back and fill them in with various patterns. Work extra rows of stitching to accentuate the shapes and do little cross hatch doodles and zigzag stitching across the lines already stitched (Fig. 19). Build up some of the bows quite densely but leave others more as outline shapes. Change the bobbin thread to single-coloured threads at this stage to give your final stitching more impact. When you change direction the needle will leave a stronger blob of colour, which you can incorporate in the design.

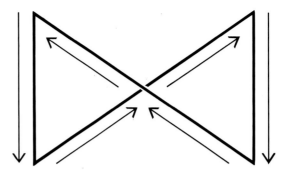

Figure 18: Use the machine needle to 'draw' bow shapes as shown.

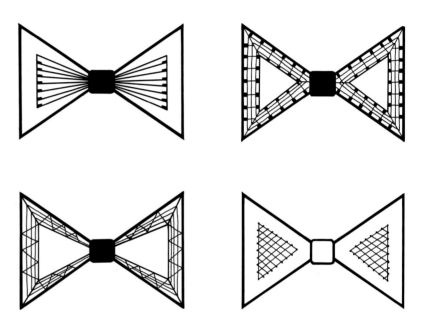

Figure 19: Fill in the bow shapes with different patterns, but leave some as simple outlines.

Work about a dozen single bows of different sizes on a separate piece of black fabric, in a small embroidery hoop or frame. Cut them out and appliqué them on top of some of the stitched bows. Attach them loosely by the centre knots, leaving the edges free to make a lovely textured cushion. Insert a zip centrally in the back of the cushion (page 39). With right sides together, stitch the back and front together, leaving the zip slightly open. Trim the seams, turn the cover to the right side and press.

ELIZABETHAN BOLSTER

This cushion uses the same Elizabethan theme and stitches as those shown on page 44.

METHOD

It can be difficult to find bolster cushion pads, but they are quite easy to make.

Take a 41 cm (16 in) square cushion pad, preferably polyester – rather than feather-filled. Roll it up, pin along the long edge and stitch by hand using strong thread.

Cut two pieces of heavyweight calico 48 x 41 cm (18 x 16 in) plus a 1.5 cm (½ in) seam

allowance. Choose a design from those shown on the Elizabethan black and white cushions on page 44, and draw the outline on the fabric. Work the embroidery through both layers of calico as described on pages 44-45, stitching the straight lines first then filling in the pattern.

For the ends of the bolster, mount a piece of calico in a 20 cm (8 in) embroidery frame. Using a compass, draw a 14 cm (5 ½ in) circle in the well of the frame.

Draw straight lines diagonally across the circle with a ruler (Fig. 20).

Remove the presser foot from the machine and slide the embroidery frame under the needle. Replace the presser foot and zigzag stitch the straight lines, and round the outline of the circle.

Fill in the centre with a stitch pattern.

Repeat for the other end of the bolster. Trim both circles to 1.5 cm (¹/₂ in) from the outer stitched circle. Machine embroider two diagonals as shown opposite. Cut them out and appliqué them to the bolster ends through their centres, with a row of satin stitching. Hand sew the tips of the diagonals to the bolster to secure.

Insert the zip down the length of the bolster (see page 39). With right sides together, ease and pin the circles to fit either end of the bolster. Tack with fairly small tacking stitching, then machine stitch. Oversew with a very small zigzag stitch to give the cover a strong finish. Trim the seams, turn to the right side and press.

The bolster cushion co-ordinates with the four cushions shown on page 38. A contrasting thread adds colour and interest, and the ends of the bolster are embellished with an appliquéd design which is machine-embroidered, cut out and applied.

Figure 20: Draw radiating lines on the bolster ends. Fill in the centres with stitch patterns.

FAN-SHAPED CUSHION

An unusual design such as this can be coordinated with cushions of different shapes to enhance existing furniture, or to give a new look to a room.

METHOD

Make a paper pattern of the cushion shape by drawing round a fan-shaped cushion pad or drawing a quarter-circle with a compass.

Cut three pieces of heavyweight calico to this shape, adding 1.5 cm (½ in) all round for seam allowances. Again choose a design from those shown on the Elizabethan black-and-white cushions on page 38. Work the embroidery throughout two layers of fabric, reserving the third piece of calico for the back of the cover. Machine embroider twenty small rectangles of calico and cut them out.

With right sides facing, place the front and back covers together. Trim the seams, turn to the right side and press. Sandwich the rectangles, so they face the cushion front, between the two curved edges and secure with machine stitching. Machine stitch one straight side.

Trim the seams, turn to the right side and press.

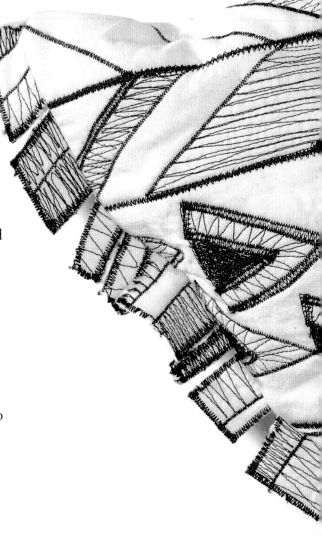

The Elizabethan theme is carried through to this fan-shaped cushion. Machine-stitched patterns in black thread contrast strongly with the calico background.

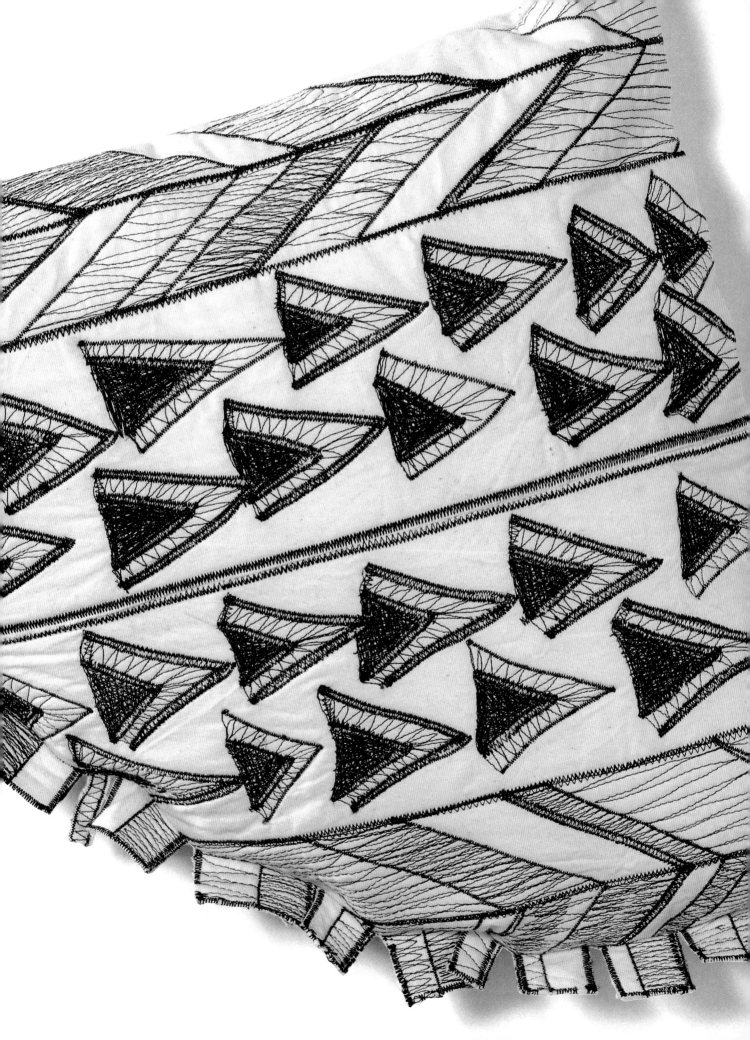

Chapter Five

Wallhanging

Chapter Five

Wallhanging

Here you can indulge your wilder fantasies of fabric and thread without constant restraints of washability and wearability being a primary concern. It is advisable, however, to use dyes or paints which are not going to fade with exposure to light. Always check the manufacturer's leaflets to see whether colours show colour-fastness to washing and dry cleaning for both natural and synthetic fibres.

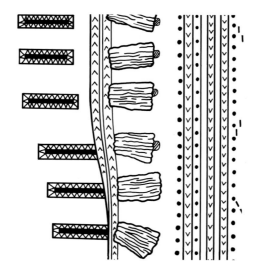

Button holes and decorative topstitching.

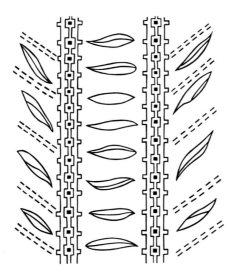

Slashed designs and braid.

DESIGNING A HANGING

No matter what subject you choose for your hanging – landscape, flowers, architecture or abstract patterns (a vast area of ideas in itself) – always start with small sketches of the things that interest you about your subject. Then try to reproduce these sketches in mixed media, paint and paper techniques, as described in Chapter 2.

My hanging is based on drawings of Elizabethan costume developed into designs on paper (see opposite and page 65). Once you start working out your ideas on paper they alter and various other ideas occur to you. This happens again when you start working with the actual fabric, so be flexible and don't stick rigidly to the plan you had at the beginning. Make decisions and solve problems as you go along – and enjoy doing it!

An example of decorative slashing.

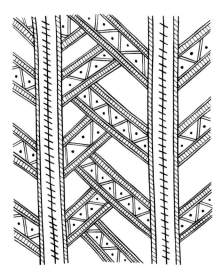

Another example of decorative slashing.

Crossbanding.

Some of the paper designs based on the drawings of Elizabethan costume.

ELIZABETHAN HANGING

The hanging is worked on cream fabric, sometimes with the addition of gold, using white or cream threads. When the embroidery is completed, the whole hanging is painted before adding the backing fabric. The completed embroidered hanging is 63.5 cm x 63.5 cm (25 x 25 in).

METHOD

The hanging is made up of quilted strips, or columns, stitched together. For each column, you need to cut three layers, each 70 cm (27 $\frac{1}{2}$ in) x the measurements given below. Use calico or silk for the top layer – I used parachute nylon as this is a very cheap, strong fabric which takes dye and paint beautifully. For the middle layer use medium-weight polyester wadding (or lightweight wadding doubled). The final layer should be lightweight calico.

First quilt the fabric for each column. Pin the three layers of fabric together and baste at approximately 5 cm (2 in) intervals, starting in the centre and working outwards. It is only necessary to baste vertically as the machine stitching at the next stage will hold the layers together. Using white Madeira 40's rayon in the top of the machine and ordinary sewing cotton in the bobbin, set the machine to a medium-width zigzag (almost satin stitch), with the presser foot on and feed dogs up. Machine stitch each column, beginning at the righthand side and with the first line of stitching 2.5 cm (1 in) from the edge.

The following instructions describe each column of the hanging separately. To save time waiting for paint to dry and constantly having to change the set-up of the sewing machine, you will find it is easiest to do each stage – printing, machine stitching, free machining and machine stitch patterns – for all the columns together.

BINDING AND FASTENING

To neaten the edges of the hanging, cut two strips of fabric 2.5 cm (1 in) x the length of the hanging and two strips x the width. With right sides facing, pin and stitch a strip of fabric to each of the two long sides. Repeat for the two shorter sides. Trim the edges to 1.5 cm ($\frac{1}{2}$ in). Fold the strips of fabric over to the wrong side of the hanging and slipstitch.

PAINTING

You will need plenty of space and time as you are now going to paint the whole hanging in one operation. Work on a large table covered with a thick layer of newspapers and clean white paper on top.

The main decision is what colours to use. You may have had a colour scheme in mind from the beginning, perhaps to match a particular room or colours you have seen in a landscape or flowers. Happy accidents of merging colours often make beautiful designs. Blue, turquoise, yellow and red Liquitex concentrated artists' colour acrylics were used for this.

Collect a few trays or tubs for mixing the paint in, a selection of paintbrushes in different sizes and a jugful of clean water. Thin the paints with water, mixing carefully until they are the consistency of runny cream.

continued on page 75

The Elizabethan wallhanging.

The inspiration for this wallhanging came from a series of studies of Elizabethan costume. Strips of cream fabric are machine stitched and embroidered over a layer of wadding and lightweight calico. The strips are sewn together and painted using a misting spray to encourage the colours to merge and blend. Each strip is called a Column and the instructions for making the wallhanging up can be found overleaf.

1   2   3   4   5   6   7

8   9   10   11   12

COLUMN I *6.5 cm (2 ¹/₂ in) wide*

1. Trace the large oblong shape in Fig. 25.
   Sponge print a design of large oblongs down
   the entire column, leaving space between each
   shape as in Fig. 26. (See page 32 for instructions on sponge printing). Use Liquitex Acrylic
   Iridiscent Gold mixed with a little water to
   thin it slightly.

2. Using the smaller oblong in Fig. 25, make a
   potato print. (See page 32 for instructions on
   potato printing). Print a small oblong in the
   centre of each sponge print, using gold mixed
   with pink acrylic.

3. Set the machine as described, using gold
   metallic thread. Stitch round each large
   sponge-printed shape as shown in Fig. 26 with
   a medium zigzag stitch. For the potato-printed
   oblongs change the thread to white Madeira
   40's rayon. Do a few back stitches to secure
   the thread before cutting it and moving on to
   the next shape.

4. Set up the machine for straight stitch free
   embroidery with the feed dogs down, the
   darning foot up, and stitch length 0 and width
   0. Fill in the background with metallic thread,
   working around and accentuating the oblong
   shapes. Alternatively, for a softer effect, use
   hand stitching.

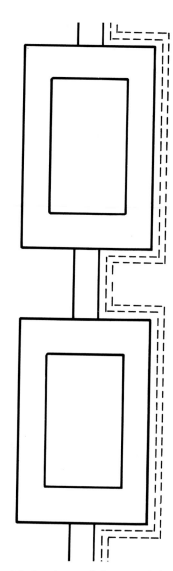

Figure 26: Stitch round the printed shapes as shown.

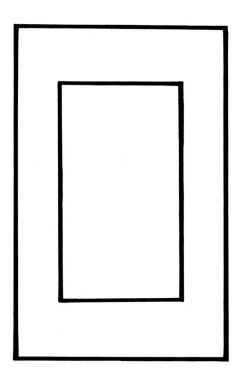

Figure 25: Printing shape for column 1 to trace off the page.

Figure 27: Trace this design.

COLUMN 2 *4 cm (1½ in) wide*

1. Trace the design in Fig. 27 and make a potato print. Print with gold Liquitex diluted as in step 1; Column 1. Leave a little space between each print as shown in Fig. 26.

2. Set the machine as above, using gold metallic thread. Stitch around each square shape and diagonally across, outlining the triangles.

3. Set the machine for free machining as step 4, but instead of straight stitch it to a wide zigzag. Using white Madeira 40's rayon, stitch between and around the square shapes (Fig. 28). Practise on a scrap of fabric first if you need to.

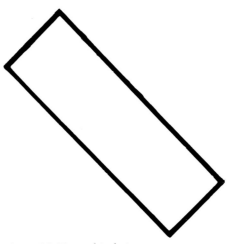

Figure 29: Trace this design.

Figure 28: Outline the shapes with free machine stitching.

COLUMN 3 *6.5 cm (2½ in)*

1. Stitch a gold 'twinkle' fabric or chiffon over the whole column.
2. Trace the design in Fig. 29. Sponge print a chevron pattern on to the gold fabric, using fold and pink Liquitex (Fig. 30).

3. Set the machine for a medium-width zigzag. Using a metallic thread on the top of the machine, stitch round each shape.

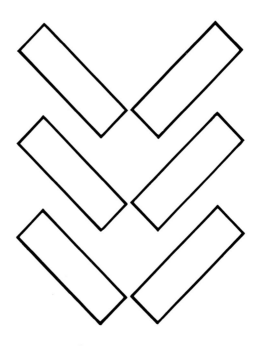

Figure 30: Chevron pattern.

COLUMN 4 *4 cm (1½ in)*

1. Tear and pleat strips of calico or silk to cover the length of the column. Machine stitch in place.

2. Trace the smaller oblong in Fig. 25 and make a potato print. Print as in column 1, but placing the oblong shape at an angle (see Fig. 31).

3. Cut small strips of squared canvas and paint gold. Apply a strip in the centre of each oblong as shown in Fig. 31 overleaf.

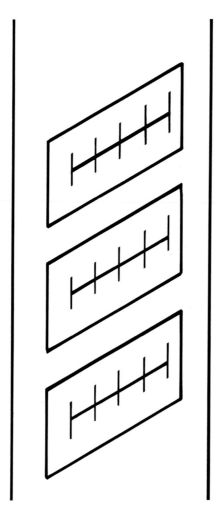

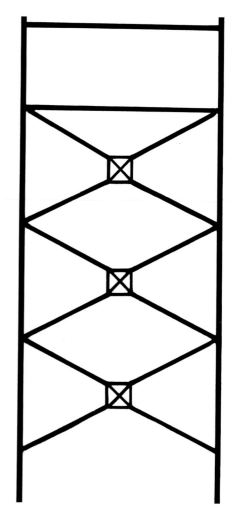

Figure 31: Stitch a strip of gold-painted canvas in the centre of each oblong.

Figure 32: Wrap a piece of fabric round each cut section to make a bow.

COLUMN 5 *4 cm (1 ¹/₂ in)*

1. Tear and pleat strips of calico or silk to cover the length of the column. Machine stitch in place.

2. Trace the smaller oblong in Fig. 25 and make a potato print. Print as in column 1, but placing the oblong shape at an angle (Fig. 31).

COLUMN 6 *5 cm (2 in)*

1. This column is not printed. Cutting through the top layer of fabric only, cut straight lines across the width of the column 3 cm (1 ¹/₄ in) apart as shown in Fig. 32.

2. Tear long strips of fabric. These can be the same as the top fabric or another similar-weight fabric.

3. Wrap a strip of fabric round each of the cut pieces as shown in Fig. 32. Tie in bow, leaving long ends.

4. Pin and tack the bows in position, then zigzag stitch down either side of the column to secure the ends of the bows.

COLUMN 7 *2.5 (1 in)*

This column is not printed.

1. Stitch two rows of pleated fabric as in column 5.

COLUMN 8 *4 cm (1 ¹/₂ in)*

1. Trace the small triangle in 33 and the oblong shape from Fig. 29. Potato print the shapes alternatively down the column as shown in Fig. 34, using gold acrylic paint.

2. Using Madeira 40's rayon in the top of the machine, outline the printed shapes in a narrow zigzag stitch.

3. Apply small scraps of torn paper (bought or handmade) to the centre of each triangle.

4. Stitch over the whole column, including the paper, in free machine zigzag.

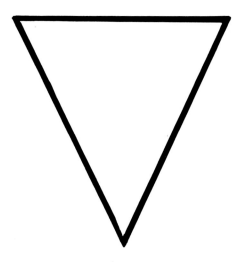

Figure 33: Trace this design.

5. Using a machine stitch pattern of your choice and a metallic or rayon thread, stitch down either side of the column.

COLUMN 9 *7 cm (2 ³/₄ in)*
1. Trace the small triangle in Fig. 33. Potato print in Liquitex gold as shown in Fig. 35, making a flower design.

2. Outline the shapes with a narrow zigzag set almost to satin stitch.

3. Fill in each triangle as shown in Fig. 35, using zigzag stitch.

4. Set the machine for free machining in straight stitch and fill in the background with random loose circles.

5. Handsew a large pearl in the centre of each flower.

COLUMN 10 *5 cm (2 in)*
Repeat the instructions for column 6 but use narrower strips of fabric for the bows. Leave the ends of the bows loose instead of stitching them down.

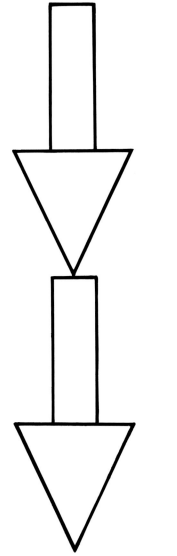

Figure 34: Position the triangles and oblongs.

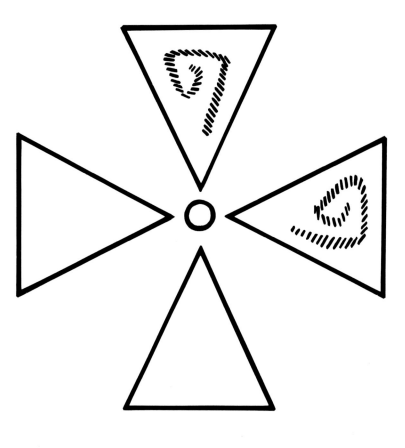

Figure 35: Flower design with pearl centre.

COLUMN 11 *6 cm (2 ½ in)*

1. Trace the large triangle in Fig. 36. Sponge print at irregular intervals down the column, using a mixture of gold and pink Liquitex paint.

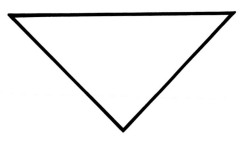

Figure 36: Printing shape for column 11 to trace off the page.

2. Outline the triangle shapes in narrow zigzag stitch, using metallic thread.

3. Set the machine for free machining in straight stitch and stitch the background in diagonal lines as shown in Fig. 38. This could be stitched by hand to give a softer effect.

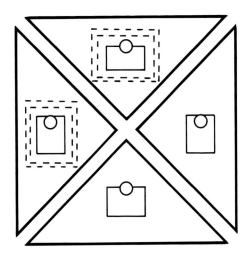

Figure 37: Outline the shapes as shown then stitch diagonal lines across the background.

COLUMN 12 *7 cm (2 ¾ in)*

1. Trace the large triangle in Fig. 36. Sponge print in Liquitex gold, positioning the triangles as shown in Fig. 37.

2. Using a small paintbrush, place a small blob of gold and pink Liquitex in the centre of each triangle (Fig. 37).

3. Outline each triangle shape in narrow zigzag stitch, using rayon thread. Stitch also round each blob of paint (Fig. 37).

4. Fill in the background in a random pattern, using rayon thread.

5. Handsew a large pearl in the centre of each blob of paint.

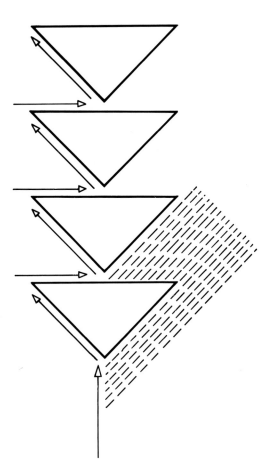

Figure 38: Stitch round each blob of paint and attach a pearl.

Spray the hanging with water, then, using the colours of your choice, start painting. Keep using the misting spray to encourage the colours to merge and spread, creating various blends of colour which will give a cohesive look to the whole hanging. Don't be tempted to use too many colours, otherwise the result can become very muddy. It is very important to finish the painting while the colours are still wet. If you leave one colour to dry and then go back and start again, it will always show.

Leave the hanging to dry flat. If you hang it up, the colour will run to the bottom although this may be the effect you want!

FINISHING

Cut a piece of calico 1.5 cm (¹/₂ in) larger all round than the finished hanging. Pin to the back of hanging, turning under the extra fabric all round.

SLIPSTITCH IN PLACE

To give you ideas for other designs and colour schemes, experiment with lino prints (see page 34). The lino blocks can be quite small as you can always enlarge the designs on a photocopier to a size suitable for a wallhanging. When you have decided on a design, work small samples in different fabrics. For a subtle effect use colours that are closely linked in the colour spectrum, or use layers or areas of bright singing colour. You can dye your own fabrics, of course, or use the cut and sew method used by Annie Rose Hemming on page 95.

Column 1 of the wallhanging

Chapter Six
Mirror Frames

Chapter Six

Mirror Frames

I have always been fascinated by frames, indeed some of them seem far more important than what they contain and pictures can be enhanced tremendously by the frame they are in. Visit an art gallery or a National Trust property to get ideas for frames – the variety is astonishing. Even churches sometimes have diptych or triptych frames which look wonderful interpreted in fabric and stitch.

This mirror frame combines two techniques – painting and machine embroidery

DESIGNING MIRROR FRAMES

If you want to use the frame for a mirror, your stitching can be as ornate as you like, perhaps using additional fabrics, stitched shapes, tassels and cords. A picture frame needs to be simpler if it is not to detract from the picture or photograph, so keep the stitching to a minimum and select the colours from the picture itself.

The sketches in Figs. 39-42 will give you some ideas and Fig. 43 contains patterns to trace. These are quartered corner sections which you can trace off the page and make into paper patterns. Enlarge or reduce them on a photocopier to fit.

To make the frames you will need card, double-sided tape and pelmet Vilene. This is the heaviest-weight Vilene available and is very rigid. Some haberdashery counters now sell wider-width pelmet Vilene or it is available by mail order. Mirror tiles tend to be very heavy and are only available in packs, so look for cheap mirrors to take apart – a picture framer may cut mirrors to size.

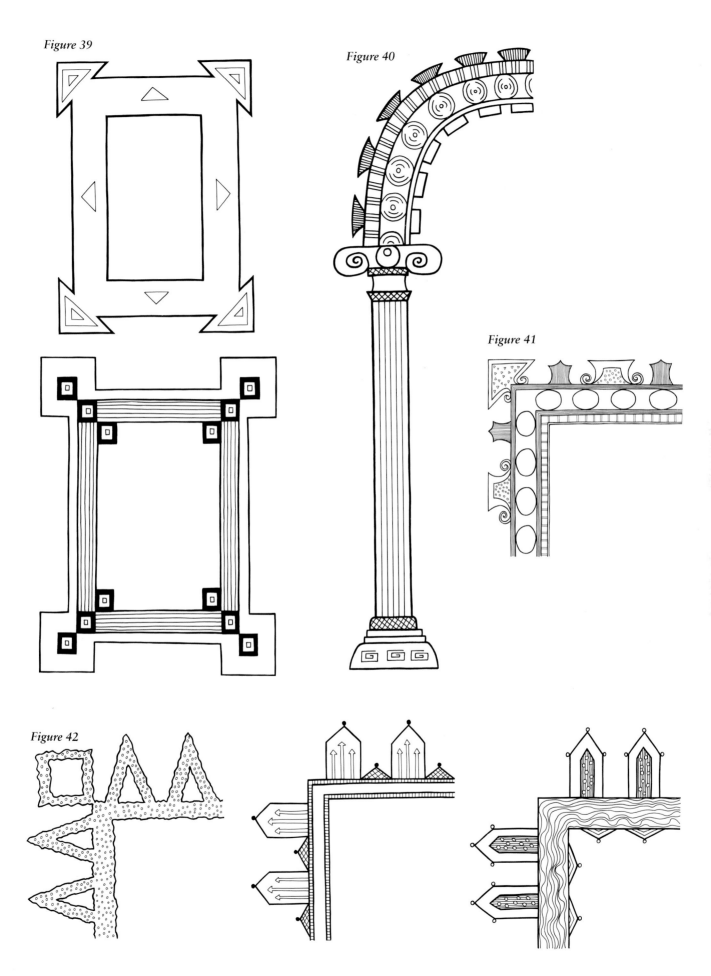

Figure 39

Figure 40

Figure 41

Figure 42

Machine-embroidered mirror frames are easy to make and very attractive. Here, silk, net, scrim and paper decorate a Vilene base. The frame is painted and machine embroidered. Tassels, bows and paper shapes are appliquéd on to the base and the frame is finished by using a zigzag stitch round all the edges.

APPLIQUÉD MIRROR FRAME

1. Trace one of the corner designs in Fig. 43 and cut out. Fold a piece of white paper in half and then in half again. Place the tracing on the folded paper and cut round the outline. Open out to give the full-size pattern.

2. Place the mirror in the centre of the paper pattern. Allowing a 1.5 cm (^{1}/$_2$ in) overlap, cut out the centre of the paper to leave room for the mirror.

3. Pin the paper pattern onto pelmet Vilene and cut out twice, cutting out the centre where the mirror will be inserted on one of the two pieces of Vilene.

4. Cut a piece of card to the size of the mirror and attach to the back of the mirror with double-sided tape. This will give the mirror a solid base but leaves the decorated corners free.

5. Take the piece of Vilene with the centre cut out – this will be the decorated top layer of the frame. Apply small pieces of silk, net, scrim, organza, even paper, using an acrylic medium to glue them in position. It does not matter if they overlap the edges of the frame as these can be trimmed later.

6. Mix small quantities of Liquitex acrylic artists' colours and paint the whole surface. This can be done while the glue is still wet.

7. Leave to dry completely then rub over the surface with a little 'Goldfinger', taking care not to obliterate the painted colour.

8. Set up the sewing machine for normal sewing, with the feed dogs up and the presser foot on. Thread with black or metallic thread on the top and black sewing cotton in the bobbin. As the frame is stiff with glue and paint, you will need a larger needle than normal, 100 or even 110.

9. Select a stitch pattern of your choice. Stitch blocks of patterning close to the inside of the frame where the mirror will be inserted and round the outer edge.

10. Decorate the frame with appliqué pieces of embroidery, using whip stitch as described for the round bow cushion on page 56. This is also a good occasion to use some of your embroidered samples, cut into scraps and applied randomly. Add a few tassels, cords, bows and paper shapes as shown in the photograph (opposite).

11. Take the backing piece of Vilene and sew a small curtain ring to the centre for hanging the mirror.

12. Lay the Vilene with the curtain ring side down and place the card-backed mirror on top. Place the decorated top layer on top to make a sandwich of the three layers. Pin the layers together at the four corners.

13. Set the machine to a medium-width zigzag, almost satin stitch, and thread with black sewing thread in both the top and the bobbin. Zigzag carefully all round the edge of the Vilene layers.

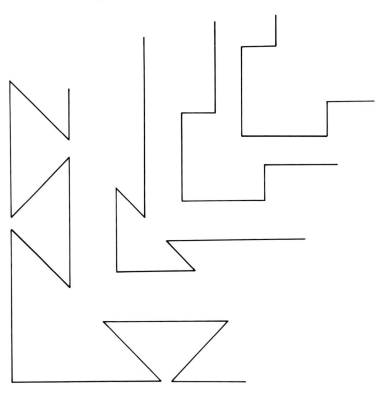

Figure 43: Various patterns for frames to trace off the page. Each pattern shows a quarter of the whole design.

Chapter Seven
Napkins & Placemats

Napkins & Placemats

Although placemats are traditionally rectangular, there is nothing to stop you making different shaped sets and they can be appliquéd, quilted or machine stitched. The placemats on pages 82-83 were worked using built-in stitch patterns. You could also use a drawn thread technique (see right). Although this is not as accurate as the hand technique, it is very pretty and easy to achieve by withdrawing three threads at regular intervals, then using a machine pattern to whip the remaining threads together. An average-size rectangular placemat is 30 x 40 cm (12 x 16 in). This could be a single layer of fabric if the surface of the table doesn't need protecting, or a three-layer quilted mat to protect the table.

A standard-size napkin is 40 cm (16 in) square, but there is no reason not to make smaller or larger ones if you prefer. The napkins and placemats in this section are made to the sizes mentioned here.

BLACKWORK BORDER

By using the set patterns on your sewing machine you can achieve an effective imitation of the lovely blackwork technique. Use an even-weave white cotton, preferably one from which you can withdraw the threads easily.

1. Cut the fabric to the size of the napkin and placemats you want, following the guidelines given above.

2. For both mats and napkins, withdraw a thread 2.5 cm (1 in) in from the outer edge all the way round. This will give you your first stitching line and will ensure that the fabric and stitching lines are straight.

3. Thread the sewing machine with black rayon thread. Set for normal stitching, with the presser foot on and feed dogs up.

4. Following the examples given in Chapter 1 or using your own combination of your own favourite machine patterns, work rows of patterning round the napkins.

Start at the line of the withdrawn thread and work inwards towards the centre. Backstitch at the beginning and end of each pattern so that the stitching doesn't come unravelled.

5. When the embroidery is complete, fringe the edges of the napkins by withdrawing the threads right up to the first row of machine stitching. If you prefer, you can hem stitch the edges.

The technique for the placemats is exactly the same. If you want a padded placemat, cut two pieces of fabric plus a layer of wadding for each mat. Tack the three layers together before starting the machine embroidery. Instead of fringing, finish the mats with a satin stitch edging and trim up to the edge. Alternatively you could use bias binding.

WHITEWORK BORDER

Use exactly the same method as for the Blackwork set but with white layer rayon thread. The rayon thread gives a lovely sheen to the stitching against white cotton fabric.

Drawn thread techniques are attractive and could be used for a set of napkins and placemats.

Machine embroidered bows are cut out and applied to black fabric. The placemats are quilted using a narrow zigzag stitch.

APPLIQUÉ BOW PATTERN

Cut the black cotton fabric on the straight of the grain, one square piece for each napkin and two oblong pieces plus wadding for each place-mat. Allow a little extra fabric for the machine appliqué bows.

Each napkin has a machine appliqué bow in one corner. The placemats have three bows down one side and two down the other.

METHOD

1. Frame a piece of black cotton fabric in a 30 cm (12 in) circular frame.

2. Trace the bows in Fig. 44 and make paper patterns. Arrange them to get the maximum number of bows within the frame Fig. 45. Don't forget that you will be working in the well of the frame!

   Using the paper templates, draw round the shapes using tailor's chalk.

3. Set the sewing machine for free machining, i.e. using a darning foot, lowering the feed dog and with stitch length 0 and width 0. Using an assortment of colours and metal threads, fill in the bow shapes with machine stitching. In this example, pink was used in the bobbin throughout the stitching. Yellow and orange were used for the first outline rows, then turquoise blue and finally pale yellow. Rayon 30's thread was used throughout.

4. When you have completely filled in the bow shapes with stitching, remove the material from the frame and cut out the bows as close to the stitching as possible.

NAPKINS

To apply a bow with tails to one corner of each napkin, first pin and tack in place. Use satin with black thread in the bobbin and through the top of the machine still with the sewing machine set for free machining but this time zigzag instead of straight stitch. Stitch all round the edges of each bow.

Finish the napkins by hemming the edges.

PLACEMATS

Place a top layer of black fabric on the wadding and tack in place. Set the machine for normal stitching i.e. presser foot on, feed dog up and set to a narrow zigzag. Quilt lines approximately 3.5 cm (1¼ in) apart diagonally across the placemats. Use black thread or a colour which matches the bows.

Taking the cut-out bow shapes, pin and tack them to the mats. Stitch in position, again with the machine set to free machine zigzag.

Pin and tack the bottom layer of black fabric to each placemat and satin stitch round the edge. Trim as close to the satin stitching as possible.

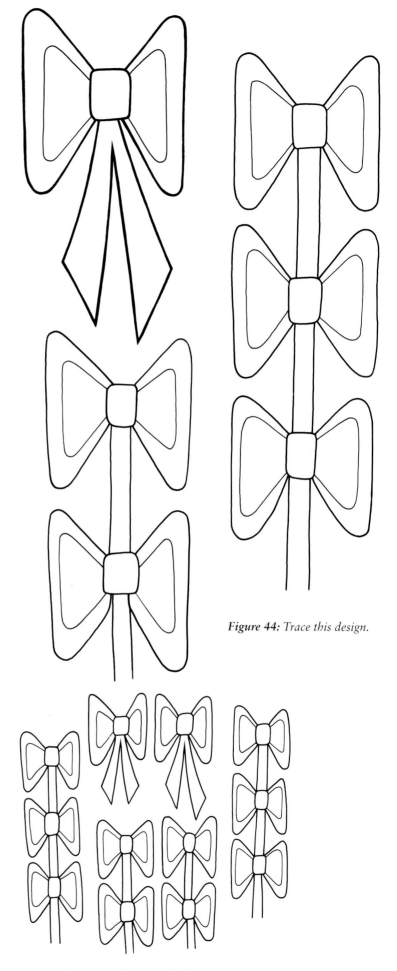

Figure 44: Trace this design.

Figure 45: Group the bows in the frame as shown for free machine stitching.

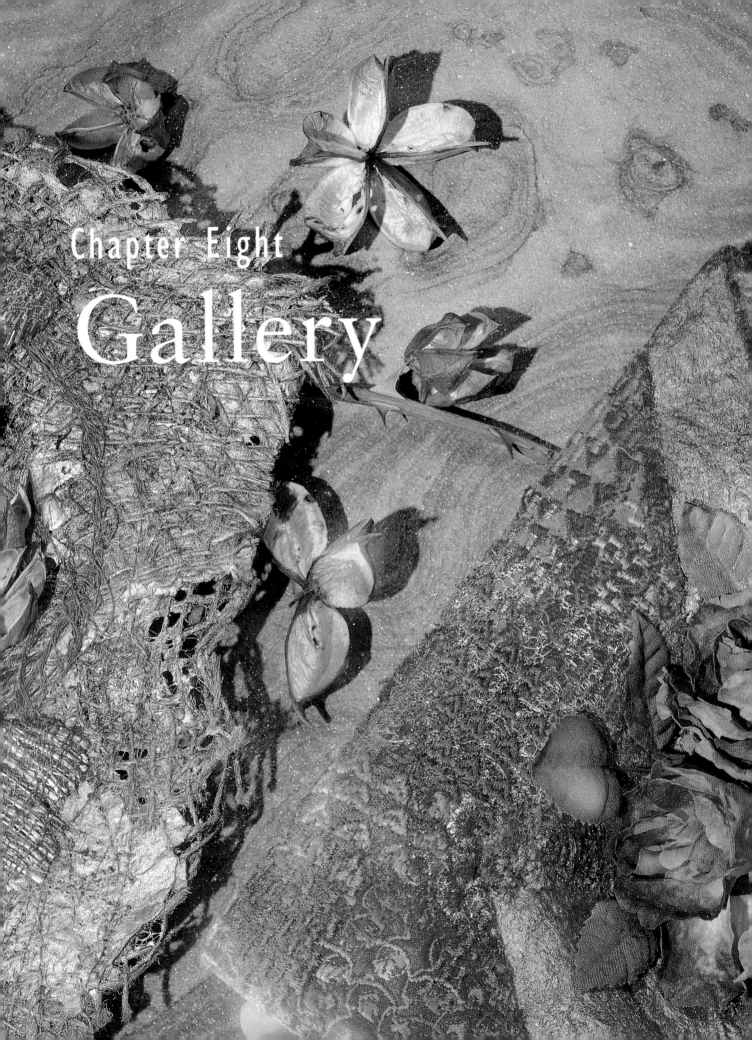

Chapter Eight

Gallery

Gallery

I have chosen a selection of work from other embroiderers to demonstrate how versatile the sewing machine can be. It is worthwhile experimenting with all the different things your machine can do, and to take your inspiration from the projects in this book, and the objects in this final chapter. The following machine embroidered objects are not functional, but they are extremely beautiful decorative objects. They all have a purpose or message that the artist wishes to express through them and, as such, I believe, are works of art which we should have in our houses to admire and look at simply because they give pleasure.

Paper, felt and a heart-shaped design are used to make these moulded bowls.

HEART BOWLS

Margaret Charlton

Margaret Charlton's Heart Bowls (see opposite) are designed to combine the heart shape and heart patterns with the square.

They are made from squares of fabric or handmade paper and layers of felt. The felt was soaked with PVA and then moulded on to glass bowls; some have aluminium mesh in them to support the shape even more. The applied heart motifs and areas of pattern were worked in machine embroidery, using free machining and stitch patterns. Each bowl was stitched by machine round the rim and the edge to hold it together. Finally the bowls were sprayed with gold and coloured inks and paints to give the metallic effect.

HEART BOXES

Margaret Charlton

A set of six small boxes in which the curved heart shape contrasts with the geometric cube; each box has a heart shape cut out of it in a different position. They are made out of pelmet Vilene painted black using fabric paint. Applied areas of red silk, sprayed gold and machine stitching in whip stitch give a rich effect on the outside to contrast with the black interiors.

Using the heart-shaped theme, pelmet Vilene is painted and red silk is applied then decorated with machine stitching.

A variety of fabric and threads, hand-made paper, metallic fabric and powders are used to create this silver vessel.

CAT CONTAINER

Margaret Charlton

Margaret's design for this was created on the computer and derives from Ancient Peruvian textiles and ceramics. The vessel was worked in three layers of fabric and machine stitching, with cat faces on both sides. After stitching the sides together and adding the base, it was painted with PVA and varnish, which gives it its rigidity and shiny surface, like beautifully worn leather.

Layers of fabric and machine stitching are covered with glue and varnish to give a textured look.

ALCHEMIST'S VESSELS

Penny Burnfield

Inspiration comes from Penny Burnfield's research into alchemy, in particular the vessel in which the alchemist makes the philosopher's stone from base matter. It is traditionally described as being egg-shaped. Penny started by studying decaying metals – iron, copper with verdigris and tarnished silver. She also studied ancient pots and ritual vessels in the British Museum.

The materials used in her pieces include felt, metallic fabric, nets, organzas and black cotton on a base of twill. Handmade paper is incorporated together with card aluminium mesh, wire and dowelling. Sections are coloured with paints, bronze powders and gold leaf. Stitch patterns and free machining are used, and many different threads, including knitting wools and metallic knitting ribbon. The techniques include couching and machine embroidery on dissolvable fabric.

Penny is currently studying textiles at Winchester School of Art. She has recently become a member of the Practical Study Group.

ZEBRA PANEL
Siân Martin

For many years Siân Martin has enjoyed the techniques of wrapping, using straws, wooden and balsa dowelling, perspex tubes and rods. Her work is based on the theme of conservation of the seas, including the preservation of whales, dolphins and other water-based wildlife. Several visits to Africa, and in particular to East Africa, have interested her in the conservation of endangered wildlife there, as a result of which Siân sponsors a baby elephant and her husband a young black rhino. The fabulous range of visual inspiration in nature has encouraged Siân to use materials new to her, such as beads, raffia and metal. Influenced by animal shapes and markings, the vast landscape and colours, and the customs of the people, she has just started to make small statements about Africa.

Using the dried texture of the landscape and the ubiquitous zebra as initial images, she has made a square frame of wrapped wooden dowelling to represent the small villages, as well as the larger protective National Park areas. Within this, the opportunity to do some 'real embroidery', as Siân calls it, presents itself. She uses both hand and machine stitchery, incorporating beads and small areas of manipulated fabric. The frames are wrapped to maintain the theme, using frayed calico and burnt silk overwrapped with raffia and cotton threads.

Siân is a member of The '62 Group of Textile Artists and teaches widely.

Hand and machine embroidery decorate this zebra panel.

Silk and organza are machine stitched together using metallic thread.

are applied to turquoise silk with black fringed fabric underneath, and attached with satin stitch. Each square is then frayed to show the coloured edges.

For the small squares layers of black felt, silk and a small coloured felt square are used. These are stitched through diagonally, with satin stitch round the edge. The fabrics are cut and trimmed close to the stitching then satin stitched again. The hanging rod is covered in the same techniques as the large squares, but worked in one long piece. Tassels at the bottom complete the effect.

WALLHANGING

Annie Rose Hemming

This lovely hanging by Annie Rose Hemming is made in beautiful Indian silks, chiffons, lurex and lawn, without the need for paints or dyes. She finds it is important to use loosely woven natural fibres, as man-made fibres do not tease out very well. In this design she has used simple triangles and squares to great effect. Three brightly coloured strips of fabric are cut on the bias and applied to the background fabric with straight stitch, following the grain of the fabric. More layers of strips are applied, to build up the squares and triangles of contrasting colours. The strips are then teased out with a wire suede brush, bringing the lower colours to the surface.

WALLHANGING

Jan Hay

Squares are applied on to a black cotton background in layers – first purple silk, then a multicolored layer of red, yellow and green silk, black silk, organza, and finally a small fringed square. The layers are stitched through in close parallel lines of machine stitching, using metallic thread. They are then cut and trimmed close to the stitching, with care taken not to cut through the bottom layer of fabric. The squares

__Opposite__ This colourful wall hanging is based on simple geometric shapes.

INDEX